21st Century Junior Library

Apatosaurus

by Lucia Raatma

CHERRY LAKE PUBLISHING * ANN ARBOR, MICHIGAN

Published in the United States of America by Cherry Lake Publishing
Ann Arbor, Michigan
www.cherrylakepublishing.com

Content Adviser: Gregory M. Erickson, PhD, Dinosaur Paleontologist,
Department of Biological Science, Florida State University, Tallahassee, Florida

Reading Adviser: Marla Conn, Read with Me Now

Photo Credits: Cover and pages 4 and 14, ©Linda Bucklin/Shutterstock, Inc.; page 6, ©Catmando/
Shutterstock, Inc.; page 8, ©iStockphoto.com/danku; page 10, ©Universal Images Group Limited/
Alamy; page 12, ©iStockphoto.com/Gloda; page 16, ©STT0007845/Media Bakery; page 18,
©Eye Risk/Alamy; page 20, ©ASSOCIATED PRESS

LIBRARY OF CONGRESS CATALOGING-IN-PUBLICATION DATA
Raatma, Lucia.
  Apatosaurus/by Lucia Raatma.
    p. cm.—(21st century junior library. Dinosaurs)
  Includes bibliographical references and index.
  ISBN 978-1-61080-463-9 (lib. bdg.)—ISBN 978-1-61080-550-6 (e-book)—
ISBN 978-1-61080-637-4 (pbk.)
  1. Apatosaurus—Juvenile literature. I. Title.
  QE862.S3R328 2013
  567.913'8—dc23   2012003503

*Cherry Lake Publishing would like to acknowledge the work of
The Partnership for 21st Century Skills.
Please visit www.21stcenturyskills.org for more information.*

Printed in the United States of America
Corporate Graphics Inc.
July 2012
CLFA11

CONTENTS

5 What Was an *Apatosaurus*?

9 What Did an *Apatosaurus* Look Like?

15 How Did an *Apatosaurus* Live?

22 Glossary

23 Find Out More

24 Index

24 About the Author

The *Apatosaurus* was one of the largest
animals of its time.

What Was an *Apatosaurus*?

Imagine a dinosaur with a huge body. It has a small head and a long tail. That is an *Apatosaurus*. It lived about 150 million years ago. It was one of the largest land animals ever! Today, all types of dinosaurs are **extinct**.

Scientists believe *Apatosaurus*es lived in groups.

The *Apatosaurus* is the same as the *Brontosaurus*. Scientists originally found two skeletons. They thought the skeletons were from different kinds of dinosaurs. So they gave each animal its own name. But the skeletons were actually the same animal! *Apatosaurus* means "deceptive lizard." *Deceptive* means able to fool.

Think!

Imagine that you are a scientist. You are studying animals that no longer live on Earth. How would you tell different types of animals apart? And how would you decide on names for them?

Apatosaurus had a long neck and tail.

What Did an *Apatosaurus* Look Like?

The *Apatosaurus* was big. It was 70 to 90 feet (21 to 27 meters) long. The top of its back was around 15 feet (4.6 m) high. The *Apatosaurus* could hold its head about 17 feet (5.2 m) high. The dinosaur weighed around 30 tons. That's about as much as three school buses!

The *Apatosaurus*'s head was very small
compared to its body.

The *Apatosaurus* was huge, but its head was small. In fact, its head was only about 2 feet (0.6 m) long. Its brain was about the size of an apple. Its teeth were like little pencils. This dinosaur had **nostrils** on top of its head. No one is sure why its nostrils were located there.

Look!

Stand in front of a full-length mirror. Look at the size of your head. Now compare it to the size of your whole body. That huge *Apatosaurus* sure had a tiny head!

It would be dangerous to be caught under an *Apatosaurus*'s heavy legs.

The *Apatosaurus* had thick, heavy legs. Each one was about the size of a large tree trunk. This dinosaur had tough skin, which helped protect it from **predators**. It had a long neck. Its long tail could whip back and forth.

Create!

Go into your yard or a nearby park. Take a tape measure with you. Measure around the trunks of a few trees. Make a chart that compares the smallest to the largest. Imagine how big an *Apatosaurus*'s leg was!

The *Apatosaurus* might have stood on its back legs
to reach treetops.

How Did an *Apatosaurus* Live?

The *Apatosaurus* was an **herbivore**. That means it ate only plants. It **grazed** on ferns, bushes, sticks, tree leaves, and pinecones. Its long neck helped it reach into a **grove** of trees to feed. However, its neck was not like a giraffe's. It reached forward, not up into the air.

Rocks helped an *Apatosaurus* digest food as the dinosaur moved around.

How much do you chew your food before swallowing? The *Apatosaurus* did not chew at all! It ate its food whole. It also swallowed rocks to help **digest** the food. As the dinosaur moved around, the rocks bounced in its stomach. Its stomach also churned, or moved, the food. This helped break down the food.

Make a Guess!

How big do you think the rocks were that an *Apatosaurus* ate? Do you think they were little stones? Or were they big boulders? Make a guess. Ask a parent, teacher, or librarian for help finding the answer. Did you guess correctly?

The *Apatosaurus* could use its tail like a whip to hit enemies.

Can you picture a huge creature plodding along? That's what the *Apatosaurus* did. It moved slowly on its heavy feet. To protect itself, it would swing its heavy tail around. This helped keep meat-eating dinosaurs away.

Ask Questions!

Next time you visit a zoo, look at the animals. What body parts help protect them from other animals? Ask zoo workers about how your favorite animal stays safe.

This scientist is studying the fossils of a young *Apatosaurus*.

The *Apatosaurus* lived in the western areas of North America. How do we know? Scientists have found its **fossils** in Colorado and other western states. The fossil of one *Apatosaurus* is on display in Pittsburgh, Pennsylvania. By studying fossils, scientists can learn about how dinosaurs lived.

GLOSSARY

digest (dye-JEST) to break down food so the body can use it

extinct (ek-STINGKT) describing a type of plant or animal that has completely died out

fossils (FAH-suhlz) the preserved remains of living things from thousands or millions of years ago

grazed (GRAYZD) fed on low-growing plants

grove (GROHV) a group of trees growing together

herbivore (HUR-buh-vor) an animal that eats plants rather than other animals

nostrils (NOSS-truhlz) the opening through which air passes when an animal smells or breathes

predators (PRED-uh-turz) animals that live by hunting other animals for food

FIND OUT MORE

BOOKS

Gray, Susan Heinrichs. *Apatosaurus*. Mankato, MN: The Child's World, 2010.

Mara, Wil. *Apatosaurus*. New York: Children's Press, 2012.

WEB SITES

American Museum of Natural History: Fossil Halls—Apatosaurus
www.amnh.org/exhibitions/ permanent/fossilhalls/vertebrate/ specimens/apatosaurus.php
Read about the *Apatosaurus* fossil on exhibit.

Carnegie Museum of Natural History: Dinosaurs in Their Time
www.carnegiemnh.org/exhibitions/ dinosaurs.html
Learn about all sorts of dinosaurs at this museum.

INDEX

B
brain, 11
Brontosaurus, 7

D
digestion, 17

E
extinction, 5

F
feet, 19
food, 15, 17
fossils, 21

G
grazing, 15

H
head, 5, 9, 11
height, 9
herbivores, 15
home, 21

L
legs, 13
length, 9, 13, 15

N
name, 7
neck, 13, 15
nostrils, 11

P
predators, 13, 19

R
rocks, 17

S
sizes, 5, 9, 11, 13
skin, 13
stomach, 17

T
tail, 5, 13, 19
teeth, 11

W
weight, 9

ABOUT THE AUTHOR

Lucia Raatma has written dozens of books for young readers. She and her family live in the Tampa Bay area of Florida. They enjoy looking at the dinosaur fossils at the local science museum.